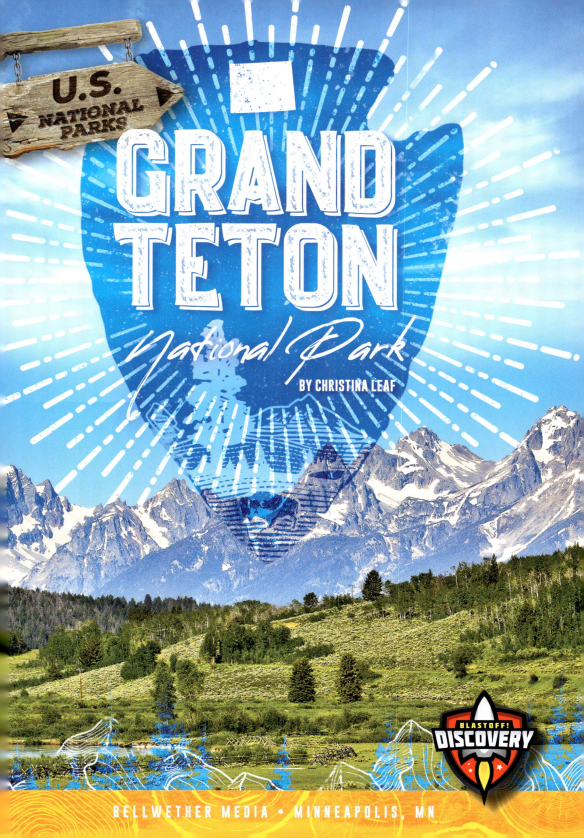

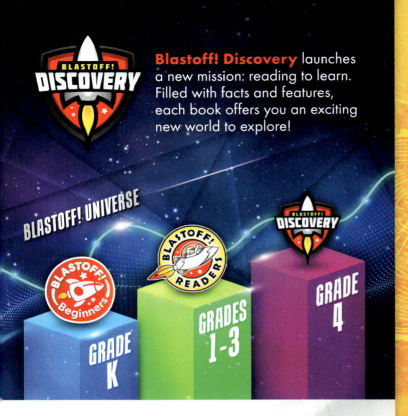

This edition first published in 2024 by Bellwether Media, Inc.

No part of this publication may be reproduced in whole or in part without written permission of the publisher.
For information regarding permission, write to Bellwether Media, Inc., Attention: Permissions Department,
6012 Blue Circle Drive, Minnetonka, MN 55343.

Library of Congress Cataloging-in-Publication Data

Names: Leaf, Christina, author.
Title: Grand Teton National Park / by Christina Leaf.
Description: Minneapolis, MN : Bellwether Media, Inc., 2024. | Series: Blastoff! Discovery : U.S. national parks | Includes bibliographical references and index. | Audience: Ages 7-13 | Audience: Grades 4-6 | Summary: "Engaging images accompany information about Grand Teton National Park. The combination of high-interest subject matter and narrative text is intended for students in grades 3 through 8"– Provided by publisher.
Identifiers: LCCN 2023045223 (print) | LCCN 2023045223 (ebook) | ISBN 9798886878134 (library binding) | ISBN 9798886879070 (ebook)
Subjects: LCSH: Grand Teton National Park (Wyo.)–Juvenile literature.
Classification: LCC F767.T3 L43 2024 (print) | LCC F767.T3 (ebook) | DDC 978.7/55–dc23/eng/20231002
LC record available at https://lccn.loc.gov/2023045223
LC ebook record available at https://lccn.loc.gov/2023045224

Text copyright © 2024 by Bellwether Media, Inc. BLASTOFF! DISCOVERY and associated logos are trademarks and/or registered trademarks of Bellwether Media, Inc.

Editor: Rebecca Sabelko
Series Design: Jeffrey Kollock   Book Designer: Laura Sowers

Printed in the United States of America, North Mankato, MN.

TABLE OF CONTENTS

A Snake River Float	4
Grand Teton National Park	6
The Land	8
Plants and Wildlife	12
Humans in Grand Teton National Park	16
Visiting Grand Teton National Park	22
Protecting the Park	24
Grand Teton National Park Facts	28
Glossary	30
To Learn More	31
Index	32

A SNAKE RIVER FLOAT

SNAKE RIVER

A family is ready for a day of floating in Grand Teton National Park! The water of the Snake River sparkles in the summer sun. In the distance, the sharp peaks of the Teton Range stand tall. The family climbs into a sturdy raft and begins to paddle.

The river winds gently through the park. It takes the family past wildflower-filled meadows and under shady cottonwood trees. They float past a pair of trumpeter swans. Later, they spy a moose searching for plants to eat. Grand Teton National Park is full of wonders!

GRAND TETON NATIONAL PARK

Grand Teton National Park is in northwestern Wyoming. It is dominated by the Teton Range. This majestic range is part of the Rocky Mountains. Grand Teton is the highest point in the range and the park. The park is named after this mountain. The eastern part of the park lies in the Jackson Hole valley.

Grand Teton covers 484 square miles (1,254 square kilometers). It lies just south of Yellowstone National Park. The city of Jackson sits just south of the park.

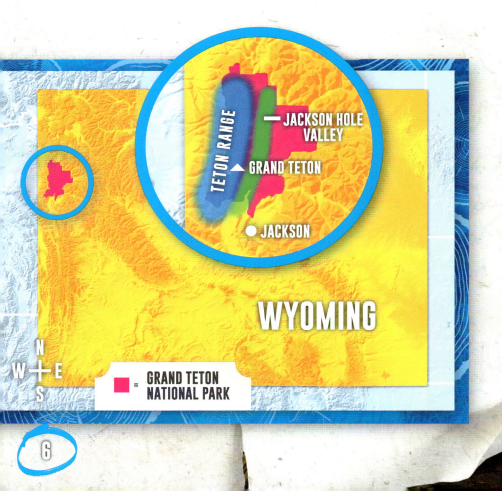

THE LAND

ON THE UP AND UP

The Tetons are still rising! One area of the park has moved about 1 foot (0.3 meters) every 100 years.

The Tetons are a very young range. Less than 10 million years ago, a **fault** in the earth's **crust** began to move. This caused many earthquakes. After each earthquake, one side of the fault was pushed up while the other side moved down. The side that pushed up formed the Tetons. The other side became Jackson Hole valley.

Erosion wears down mountains over time, giving older ranges a rounded look. The young Tetons have had less time to erode. This is why they still have sharp, jagged peaks. Some erosion has happened, though. **Glaciers** carved some valleys into U shapes.

FORMING THE TETONS

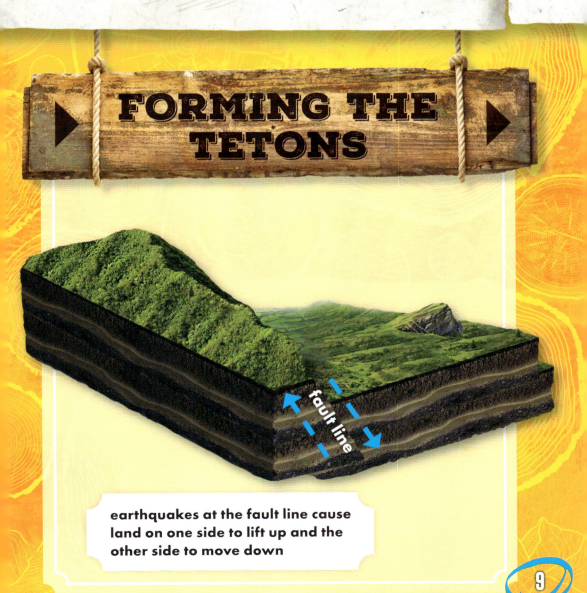

earthquakes at the fault line cause land on one side to lift up and the other side to move down

The Teton Range runs along the park's western edge. Grand Teton peak towers near the center of the range. Small lakes trail down the eastern side of the mountains. Jackson Lake covers much of the park's north. The mighty Snake River flows through Jackson Hole valley in the eastern part of the park.

AVERAGE TEMPERATURES

JANUARY
- HIGH: 26°F (-3°C)
- LOW: 1°F (-17°C)

APRIL
- HIGH: 49°F (9°C)
- LOW: 22°F (-6°C)

JULY
- HIGH: 81°F (27°C)
- LOW: 42°F (6°C)

OCTOBER
- HIGH: 56°F (13°C)
- LOW: 23°F (-5°C)

°F = degrees Fahrenheit   °C = degrees Celsius

Grand Teton has four seasons. Winter is cold and snowy. Spring is cool with both rain and snow. Most rain falls in summer. Thunderstorms often roll in on hot summer afternoons. Fall is usually sunny but cool. The mountains are colder than the valley floor.

PLANTS AND WILDLIFE

Grand Teton is filled with life! In Jackson Hole valley, pronghorns nibble on sagebrush. Elk and bison graze on grasses. Sage-grouse and sagebrush lizards dart through tall grasses. Coyotes chase ground squirrels. Summer wildflowers such as Indian paintbrushes, lupines, and larkspurs add bursts of color.

Many animals rely on the park's waters. Beavers build homes from sticks while frogs call from ponds. Moose search for water lilies in lakes and willows along rivers. Tiger salamanders rest near streams. Cottonwoods and poplars line the Snake River where cutthroat trout swim. Bald eagles circle overhead, looking for a meal.

GREATER SAGE-GROUSE

SAGEBRUSH LIZARD

BOREAL CHORUS FROG

GRAY WOLF

COMEBACK STORY

Long ago, gray wolves were hunted until no more lived in the area around Grand Teton. They were reintroduced in the mid-1990s. Today, six packs live in the park.

MOOSE

Life Span: around 15 to 20 years
Status: least concern

moose range =

| LEAST CONCERN | NEAR THREATENED | VULNERABLE | ENDANGERED | CRITICALLY ENDANGERED | EXTINCT IN THE WILD | EXTINCT |

BLACK BEAR

FORGET-ME-NOTS

On the mountain peaks, pikas squeak from rock piles while marmots look out for danger. Forget-me-nots speckle the rocky land. Bighorn sheep easily walk the steep slopes. Golden eagles soar above the peaks.

GOLDEN EAGLE

Mountain lions weave through forests of lodgepole pines on low mountain slopes, hunting for small mammals. Western tanagers make nests in the tall trees. Grizzly and black bears pluck huckleberries from branches. Swallowtail butterflies flit through meadows of fireweed and mountain bluebells.

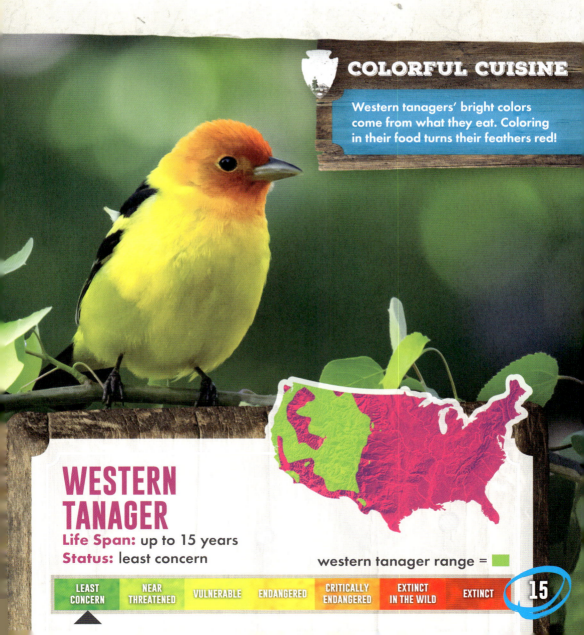

COLORFUL CUISINE

Western tanagers' bright colors come from what they eat. Coloring in their food turns their feathers red!

WESTERN TANAGER

Life Span: up to 15 years
Status: least concern

western tanager range =

| LEAST CONCERN | NEAR THREATENED | VULNERABLE | ENDANGERED | CRITICALLY ENDANGERED | EXTINCT IN THE WILD | EXTINCT |

HUMANS IN GRAND TETON NATIONAL PARK

The first humans arrived in Grand Teton National Park at least 11,000 years ago. They were following animals to hunt. By the 1800s, many different Native American nations used the area. They included the Shoshone, Blackfoot, Crow, Gros Ventre, Bannock, and Flathead. Most of the groups were **nomadic**. In warmer months, they hunted animals and gathered resources in the area. The mountains held spiritual meaning for many of the nations.

The first recorded European to come through the area was John Colter. He arrived in the early 1800s as part of the **Lewis and Clark expedition**.

Fur trappers and traders arrived next. In 1872, an expedition **surveyed** the area. The group is believed to have been the first Europeans to reach the peak of Grand Teton. **Homesteaders** moved into the area in the late 1800s, including **Mormons** in the 1890s.

In the early 1900s, **tourists** started visiting to experience the cowboy lifestyle. New buildings and other development sprung up all over the area. Local people grew concerned. They worried the development would ruin the wilderness. After visiting the area and speaking with locals, oil **tycoon** John D. Rockefeller agreed to help protect the land.

LAST HOMESTEAD CABINS IN JACKSON HOLE

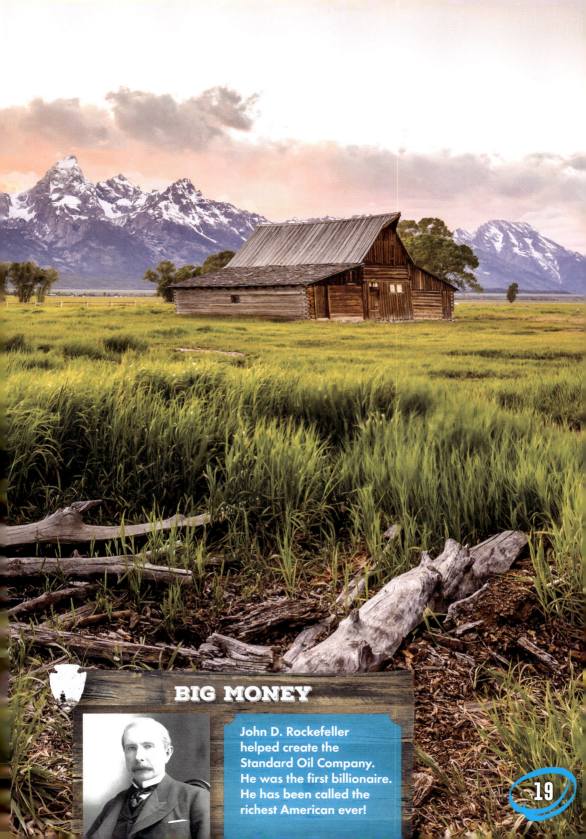

BIG MONEY

John D. Rockefeller helped create the Standard Oil Company. He was the first billionaire. He has been called the richest American ever!

In 1929, President Calvin Coolidge signed the law creating Grand Teton National Park. The park only included the mountains and nearby lakes. However, Rockefeller had secretly been using his wealth to buy land around the park. It took many years, but that land became part of the park in 1950.

PRESIDENT CALVIN COOLIDGE

ANSEL ADAMS PHOTO OF THE TETONS AND THE SNAKE RIVER

THE BIG PICTURE

Many people connect photographer Ansel Adams with the park. He snapped a photo of the Tetons and the Snake River. It became famous! Many people try to recreate this photo today.

Today, nearly 3 million people visit Grand Teton each year. They can learn about the park's history by visiting historic buildings. Park staff educate visitors about the Native American nations in the area. They honor the land's original caretakers.

VISITING GRAND TETON NATIONAL PARK

Grand Teton offers many different activities! In warmer months, boaters get out on the water in canoes, kayaks, and rafts. Anglers cast for trout in the park's many lakes. Hikers take trails up into the mountains. Rock climbers scale the highest peaks. Wildlife lovers look for moose, elk, and other animals.

TOP SITES

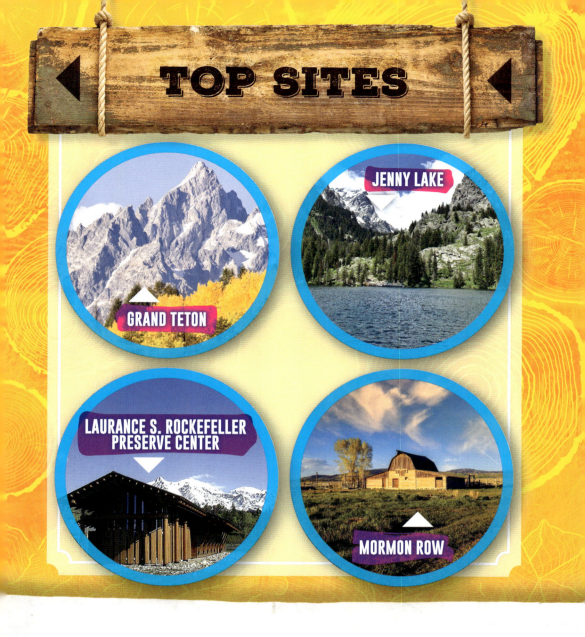

Winter offers even more ways to enjoy the park. People wait for fish to bite while ice fishing on frozen Jackson Lake. Visitors trek through the park on cross-country skis or snowshoes. Some snowboarders and downhill skiers search for powder in the backcountry. Grand Teton is fun year-round!

PROTECTING THE PARK

Grand Teton faces many threats. **Invasive species** come into the park and take the place of species that belong. This harms the **ecosystems**. Park staff work to keep invasive species contained. They remove unwanted weeds and check boats to keep lakes and rivers safe. They try to reestablish the original species.

Climate change is causing more wildfires, melting the park's glaciers, and destroying animal **habitats**. Park staff work to combat climate change with clean energy. One example is the Laurance S. Rockefeller Preserve Center. It uses clean energy while also teaching about **conservation**.

INVASIVE SPECIES

WILDFIRE DAMAGE

Nearby oil and gas drilling could become another threat. It would harm the wildlife by changing their **migration** patterns. Some groups are speaking out to keep drilling away from the park.

MIGRATING BIRDS

In 2013, a conservation group helped pass a bill to add land to the park. This stopped the land from being used for houses and hotels, which would disturb wildlife and the park's ecosystems. People want to keep Grand Teton National Park beautiful for future **generations**!

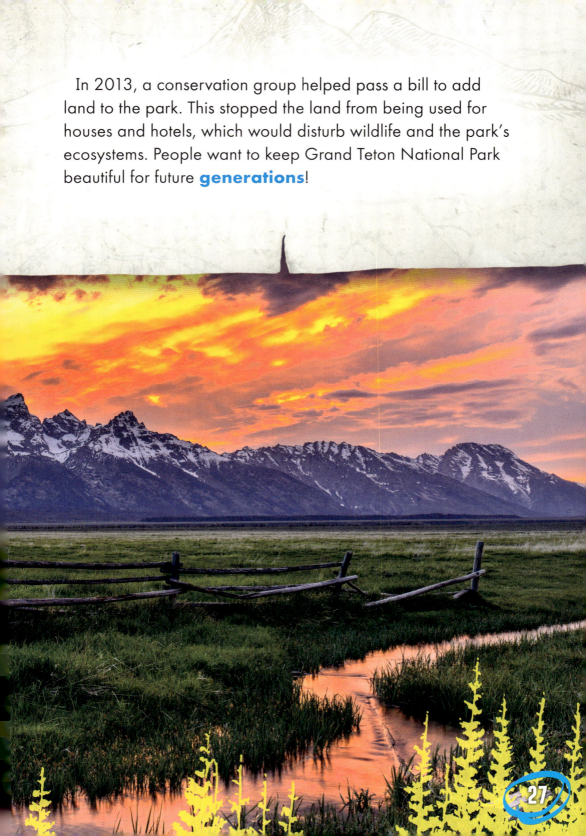

GRAND TETON NATIONAL PARK FACTS

Area: **484** square miles
(1,254 square kilometers)

Annual Visitors:
2,806,223 visitors in 2022

Area Rank: 25TH
largest park

Population Rank: 12TH
most visited park in 2022

Date Established:
February 26, 1929

Highest Point: Grand Teton;
13,775 feet (4,199 meters)

TIMELINE

PRE–
1800s
Many Native American peoples use the area

1807–1808
John Colter is the first European to visit Jackson Hole valley and the Tetons

28

FOOD WEB

GRAY WOLF

BALD EAGLE

ELK

GREATER SAGE-GROUSE

SAGEBRUSH

1890s
Mormons settle in the area, creating Mormon Row

1929
Grand Teton National Park is created

1950
John D. Rockefeller's land becomes part of the national park

29

GLOSSARY

climate change—a human-caused change in Earth's weather due to warming temperatures

conservation—the careful protection of something

crust—the outer layer of the earth's surface

ecosystems—communities of living things that include plants, animals, and the environment around them

erosion—the process through which rocks are worn away by wind, water, or ice

fault—a break in the earth's crust that separates tectonic plates; tectonic plates are large pieces of the earth's crust that are slowly moving.

generations—people who make up the steps in a line from one ancestor

glaciers—massive sheets of ice that cover large areas of land

habitats—natural homes of plants and animals

homesteaders—people who gain a piece of public land by settling on it

invasive species—plants or animals that are not originally from the area; invasive species often cause harm to their new environments.

Lewis and Clark expedition—a journey undertaken in the early 1800s to explore the new western part of the United States

migration—the act of traveling from one place to another, often with the seasons

Mormons—members of the Church of Jesus Christ of Latter-day Saints

nomadic—relating to people who have no fixed home but wander from place to place

surveyed—studied and measured an area of land

tourists—people who travel to visit a place

tycoon—a businessperson who has great wealth and power

TO LEARN MORE

AT THE LIBRARY

Bowman, Chris. *Yellowstone National Park.* Minneapolis, Minn.: Bellwether Media, 2023.

Isabella, Jude. *Bringing Back the Wolves: How a Predator Restored an Ecosystem.* Toronto, Ont.: Kids Can Press, 2020.

Payne, Stefanie. *The National Parks: Discover All 62 Parks of the United States.* New York, N.Y.: DK Publishing, 2020.

ON THE WEB

FACTSURFER

Factsurfer.com gives you a safe, fun way to find more information.

1. Go to www.factsurfer.com.

2. Enter "Grand Teton National Park" into the search box and click 🔍.

3. Select your book cover to see a list of related content.

INDEX

activities, 4, 21, 22–23
Adams, Ansel, 21
average temperatures, 11
climate, 11
climate change, 24
Colter, John, 17
Coolidge, Calvin, 20
fast facts, 28–29
glaciers, 9, 24
Grand Teton, 6, 10, 18
history, 8, 12, 16, 17, 18, 19, 20, 21, 27
invasive species, 24
Jackson, 6
Jackson Hole valley, 6, 8, 10, 11, 12, 18
Jackson Lake, 10, 23
landscape, 4, 5, 6, 7, 8, 9, 10, 11, 12, 14, 15, 16, 18, 20, 21, 22, 23, 24
Laurance S. Rockefeller Preserve Center, 24
Lewis and Clark expedition, 17
location, 6

map, 6
name, 6
people, 16, 17, 18, 19, 20, 21, 22, 23, 24, 26, 27
plants, 5, 12, 14, 15, 24
protecting the park, 18, 24, 26, 27
Rockefeller, John D., 18, 19, 20
size, 6
Snake River, 4–5, 10, 12, 21
Teton Range, 4, 6, 7, 8, 9, 10, 11, 14, 15, 16, 18, 20, 21, 22
threats, 18, 24, 26
top sites, 23
wildfires, 24, 25
wildlife, 5, 12, 13, 14, 15, 16, 22, 23, 24, 26, 27
Wyoming, 6
Yellowstone National Park, 6

The images in this book are reproduced through the courtesy of: Chanya Thirawarapan, front cover; Checubus, pp. 3, 29 (1929); blewulis, pp. 4-5; Alisa Khliestkova, p. 5 Earth Trotter Photography, pp. 6-7; Andrew Zarivny, p. 8; Sean Xu, pp. 10, 26-27; Wesley Gilson, p. 11; miroslav chytil, p. 12 (gray wolf); Tom Rechner, pp. 12 (greater sage-grouse), 29 (greater sage-grouse); Tyler Hulett, p. 12 (sagebrush lizard); AnnaC17, p. 12 (boreal chorus frog); Harry Collins Photography, p. 13 (moose); Sundry Photography, p. 14 (forget-me-nots); Michael-Tatman, p. 14 (black bear); Al Carrera, p. 14 (golden eagle); Eivor Kuchta, p. 15; Kelly vanDellen, pp. 16-17; Daniel Mayer/ Wikipedia, p. 18; f11photo, p. 19; Scientific American Compiling Dep't/ Wikipedia, p. 19 (John D. Rockefeller); Notman Studio/ Wikipdedia, p. 20 (President Calvin Coolidge); gary718, p. 20; Ansel Adams/ Wikipedia, p. 21; IrinaK, p. 22 (cross-country skiing); pchaople, p. 22 (rock climbing); Alex GK Lee, p. 23 (Grand Teton); AVM_Lens, p. 23 (Jenny Lake); Eoghanacht/ Wikipedia, p. 23 (Laurance S. Rockefeller Preserve Center); Nick Fox, p. 23 (Mormon Row); Jon G. Fuller/VWPics/ Alamy, p. 24; USFS Photo/ Alamy, pp. 24-25, 25 (wildfire damage); Kent Weakley, p. 26 (migrating birds); stacywills, p. 28 (pre-1800s); Steven Cukrov, p. 28 (1807-1808); Kaleidoscopes, p. 29 (1890s); Danielle Lehle/NPS/ Wikipedia, p. 29 (1950); Vlada Cech, p. 29 (gray wolf); Colin Edwards Wildside, p. 29 (bald eagle); Cornelius Doppes, p. 29 (elk); EQRoy, p. 29 (sagebrush); Pat Tr, pp. 28-29, 30-31, 32; Marek Mierzejewski, p. 31.